# GUERRILLA MARKETING
## 101 LAB

### LESSONS FROM THE
### FATHER OF
### GUERRILLA MARKETING

# JAY CONRAD LEVINSON
## BEST SELLING AUTHOR WITH OVER 14 MILLION BOOKS SOLD

1

# GUERRILLA MARKETING
## 101 LAB

By Jay Conrad Levinson

ISBN: 1-933596-16-3    Guerrilla Marketing 101 DVD & Workbook Bundle

ISBN: 1-933596-17-1    Guerrilla Marketing 101 DVD

ISBN: 1-933596-18-X    Guerrilla Marketing 101 Workbook

Published by:

# MORGAN · JAMES
### PUBLISHING FOR THE REST OF US...

Morgan James Publishing, LLC
1225 Franklin Ave Ste 325
Garden City, NY 11530-1693
Toll Free 800-485-4943
www.MorganJamesPublishing.com

Habitat
for Humanity®
Peninsula
Building Partner

Cover and Inside Design by:
Heather Kirk
www.GraphicsByHeather.com
Heather@GraphicsByHeather.com

# TABLE OF CONTENTS

## WORKBOOK:

WELCOME . . . . . . . . . . . . . . . . . . . . . . . . . . . . . . . . . . . . . . . . . . . . .9

INSTRUCTIONS . . . . . . . . . . . . . . . . . . . . . . . . . . . . . . . . . . . . .11

EXERCISE 1: *Your Business Goals* . . . . . . . . . . . . . . . . . . . . . .13

EXERCISE 2: *Benefits Of Doing Business With You* . . . . . . . . . . .15

EXERCISE 3: *Your Competitive Advantages* . . . . . . . . . . . . . . . .17

EXERCISE 4: *Choose Your Marketing Weapons* . . . . . . . . . . . . .19

EXERCISE 5: *Your Target Market* . . . . . . . . . . . . . . . . . . . . . .21

EXERCISE 6: *Building Consent With Soft Steps* . . . . . . . . . . . . .23

EXERCISE 7: *The 7-Sentence Marketing Plan* . . . . . . . . . . . . . .25

EXERCISE 8: *Your Creative Plan* . . . . . . . . . . . . . . . . . . . . . . .27

EXERCISE 9: *Your Media Plan* . . . . . . . . . . . . . . . . . . . . . . . .29

EXERCISE 10: *Create A Theme Line* . . . . . . . . . . . . . . . . . . . . .31

EXERCISE 11: *Meme* . . . . . . . . . . . . . . . . . . . . . . . . . . . . . . .33

EXERCISE 12: *Deploy Your Weapons* . . . . . . . . . . . . . . . . . . . .35

EXERCISE 13: *Become The Expert* . . . . . . . . . . . . . . . . . . . . . .37

EXERCISE 14: *Ask Your Customers* . . . . . . . . . . . . . . . . . . . . .39

EXERCISE 15: *Create a Referral Plan* . . . . . . . . . . . . . . . . . . . .41

EXERCISE 16: *Follow-Up* . . . . . . . . . . . . . . . . . . . . . . . . . . . .43

EXERCISE 17: *Your Magazine Ad* . . . . . . . . . . . . . . . . . . . . . .45

EXERCISE 18: *Email Your Customers* . . . . . . . . . . . . . . . . . . . .49

EXERCISE 19: *Use Postcards* . . . . . . . . . . . . . . . . . . . . . . . . . .51

EXERCISE 20: *Draft A Brochure* . . . . . . . . . . . . . . . . . . . . . . .53

**EXERCISE 21:** *Build A Web Site* . . . . . . . . . . . . . . . . . . . . . . . . . . .55

**EXERCISE 22:** *Your Guerrilla Marketing Calendar* . . . . . . . . . . . . . . . .59

**EXERCISE 23:** *What You Give For Free* . . . . . . . . . . . . . . . . . . . . . . .61

**EXERCISE 24:** *Find Fusion Marketing Partners* . . . . . . . . . . . . . . . . . .63

**EXERCISE 25:** *Give Talks* . . . . . . . . . . . . . . . . . . . . . . . . . . . . . . . .65

**EXERCISE 26:** *Your Competitors* . . . . . . . . . . . . . . . . . . . . . . . . . . .67

**EXERCISE 27:** *The Elevator Pitch* . . . . . . . . . . . . . . . . . . . . . . . . . . .69

**EXERCISE 28:** *Take Specific Action* . . . . . . . . . . . . . . . . . . . . . . . . .71

**BONUS EXERCISE 1:** *30-Second TV Commercial* . . . . . . . . . . . . . . . .73

**BONUS EXERCISE 2:** *Radio Spot* . . . . . . . . . . . . . . . . . . . . . . . . . . .77

**BONUS EXERCISE 3:** *PR Plan* . . . . . . . . . . . . . . . . . . . . . . . . . . . . .79

**BONUS EXERCISE 4:** *Create A Direct Mail Piece* . . . . . . . . . . . . . . . .83

**BONUS EXERCISE 5:** *Your Guerrilla Marketing Attack* . . . . . . . . . . . . .87

**QUIZ:** *Test Your Guerrilla Marketing Knowledge* . . . . . . . . . . . . . . . .89

**COMMON MARKETING TERMS** . . . . . . . . . . . . . . . . . . . . . . . . . .97

NEED EXTRA HELP . . . . . . . . . . . . . . . . . . . . . . . . . . . . . . . . .103

QUIZ ANSWERS . . . . . . . . . . . . . . . . . . . . . . . . . . . . . . . . . . .105

CONCLUSION . . . . . . . . . . . . . . . . . . . . . . . . . . . . . . . . . . . .109

THE COMPLETE GUERRILLA MARKETING ARSENAL . . . . . . . . .111

GET YOUR FREE BONUS GIFTS . . . . . . . . . . . . . . . . . . . . . . . . .113

\* If you purchased this *Guerrilla Marketing 101 LAB* workbook by itself and would like to purchase the entire *Guerrilla Marketing 101: Lessons from the Father of Guerrilla Marketing*, which includes 4 DVDs, visit the Morgan James Publishing Bookstore at http://www.MorganJamesPublishing.com.

# GUERRILLA MARKETING 101 LAB DVD*

## DISC CHAPTERS:

1. OPENING CREDITS

2. YOUR BUSINESS GOALS

3. YOUR BENEFITS LIST

4. COMPETITIVE ADVANTAGES

5. CHOOSE YOUR WEAPONS

6. TARGET MARKETS

7. BUILD CONSENT

8. THE SEVEN-SENTENCE G.M. PLAN

9. YOUR CREATIVE PLAN

10. YOUR MEDIA PLAN

11. CREATE A THEME LINE

12. MEME

13. DEPLOY YOUR WEAPONS!

14. BECOME THE EXPERT!

15. ASK YOUR CUSTOMERS

16. CREATE A REFERRAL PLAN

17. FOLLOW-UP!

18. YOUR MAGAZINE AD

19. EMAIL YOUR CUSTOMERS

20. USE POSTCARDS

21. DRAFT A BROCHURE

22. BUILD A WEB SITE

23. YOUR G.M. CALENDAR

24. HOW WILL YOU GIVE BACK?

25. FIND FUSION PARTNERS

26. GIVE TALKS

27. YOUR COMPETITORS

28. THE ELEVATOR PITCH

29. TAKE SPECIFIC ACTION

30. THE NEXT STEPS

*Press PREV and NEXT on your remote to access the chapters. Press PAUSE while doing the exercises.*

# GUERRILLA MARKETING 101 DVDS*

## DISC ONE CHAPTERS:

1. OPENING CREDITS

2. WELCOME!

3. A BUSINESS REVOLUTION

4. THE 20 G.M. DIFFERENCES

5. ABOUT G.M. WEAPONS

6. G.M. WEAPONS #1-51

## DISC TWO CHAPTERS:

1. G.M. WEAPONS #52-100

2. MEMES

3. SCIENCE OF G.M.

4. THE GUERRILLA PERSONALITY

5. MONUMENTAL SECRETS OF G.M.

6. G.M. ONLINE

7. THE 7-SENTENCE G.M. PLAN

## DISC THREE CHAPTERS:

1. G.M. ATTACK!

2. GUERRILLA POWERS/LIMITATIONS

3. HOW GUERRILLAS SAVE MONEY

4. Q &A WITH JAY

5. JOIN THE GMA!

6. CONCLUSION

*Press PREV and NEXT on your remote to access the chapters.*

# WELCOME

Welcome to the *Guerrilla Marketing 101 Lab*. If you have not yet viewed the *Guerrilla Marketing 101* Lecture DVDs, now is the time to do so because those discs contain the theory you need to take the actions found in this workbook. Guerrilla marketers always strive to balance theory with action. Theory guides you to the actions you need to take, and action is what makes things happen. You can't have one without the other.

This workbook is where you put your ideas into action. These pages contain exercises designed to help you create your Guerrilla Marketing system. How well will this system work? If you complete each of these exercises to the best of your ability and put everything you create into action with 100% commitment, you will have greatly increased your odds of achieving — and surpassing — your business goals.

Each exercise represents an opportunity for you to think and focus on the right questions so that you can come up with the right answers. Like any course, each exercise is timed. You'll have anywhere from 2 to 15 minutes per exercise for a total of 3 hours and 35 minutes. Unlike other courses, there is no teacher or proctor to make sure you complete your work on time. For best results, I recommend that you take as much of the allowed time as possible without cheating by going over time. No one is watching you and you are free to do whatever you want — but if you cheat, the only person you'll be cheating is yourself.

You'll get the most out of this workbook if you take it step by step, in the order presented, and with total conscientiousness. The lists you'll be asked to make will carry you forward into the marketing battle, arming you with the competence and confidence you need to fight — and win.

## THE FIVE PERCENT RULE

It is estimated that only 5% of people who attend a seminar will act on the information they learn, usually because they feel overwhelmed. They feel that they must take action immediately on absolutely everything they've been taught. Guerrilla marketers know that taking action is a gradual process that works best when undertaken in a carefully-planned series of steps. This workbook contains 28 exercises plus several bonus exercises designed to break your marketing process down into small, easy-to-manage steps.

The first step in achieving your business goals is transferring your ideas and plans from your head into printed words that you and others can read. Why? Because even the boldest ideas remain meek and hidden until translated into the written marching orders that precede a guerrilla marketing attack. You have already commenced this process by watching the *Guerrilla Marketing 101* Lecture discs. The *Guerrilla Marketing 101 Lab* capitalizes on that momentum. Keep going, step-by-step, and you'll achieve the success you want and deserve.

## GETTING THE MOST FROM THE *GM 101* COURSE

Getting the most out of *Guerrilla Marketing 101* is easy. All you have to do is treat every word and number you write as a solemn oath to yourself and to your business. Give yourself a time limit of no more than one month from today to complete the entire *Guerrilla Marketing 101* course. You may take this course alone or with one or two other people. Avoid the temptation to have too many people around you. Like their paramilitary counterparts, guerrilla marketers function most effectively either individually or as members of small, tight groups.

**TIP:** The exception to this rule is after you have completed both the *Guerrilla Marketing 101* Lecture and Lab. At that point, feel free to show the Lecture discs to your coworkers and hold immediate brainstorming sessions both between sections and at the conclusion of the program. You'll get lots of great ideas and your coworkers will appreciate being part of your business's success story.

You can complete all 28 exercises plus bonuses in 1 long day or space the exercises over several days. It's up to you. If you decide to complete all exercises in a single day and schedule that day right now, then you are truly acting in the Guerrilla Marketing spirit. Even better, if you find yourself enjoying this process, then your competitors are more than likely in serious trouble.

# INSTRUCTIONS

Here's how to complete the *Guerrilla Marketing 101 Lab*:

1) Make sure you are in a quiet place free from distractions. Have your DVD player and a timer or stopwatch ready.

2) Watch the first (or next) exercise on the *Guerrilla Marketing 101 Lab* DVD.

3) Stop or pause the DVD when prompted and set your timer to the time allotted for the current exercise.

4) Complete the exercise in the time allotted. **No cheating**.

5) After completing the exercise, you may take a break or continue. If you decide to take a break, remember that you can skip the DVD ahead to the desired chapter by pressing the NEXT button on your DVD remote.

6) Repeat Steps 1-5 for each subsequent exercise until you complete this program.

7) Take action.

Remember: The final grade you receive in this course will be measured by the profits you earn from these exercises. I wish you well with The *Guerrilla Marketing 101 Lab* and hope you graduate with honors.

# NOTES:

# EXERCISE 1: YOUR BUSINESS GOALS

Express your business goals in terms of the amount of income (profit) you want each month :and the number of days off you want each month. Do this for the first, third, and fifth years from today.

TIME: 3 MINUTES

## YEAR ONE

The amount of profit I want is $ _____ per month.

I want _____ days off per month.

## YEAR THREE

The amount of profit I want is $ _____ per month.

I want _____ days off per month.

## YEAR FIVE

The amount of profit I want is $ _____ per month.

I want _____ days off per month.

# NOTES:

# EXERCISE 2: BENEFITS OF DOING BUSINESS WITH YOU

This is an extremely important list, because here is where you list all of the benefits of doing business with your company. Don't be shy. Be sure to list every possible benefit you can think of, no matter how minor it might seem.

TIME: 5 MINUTES

## The benefits of doing business with my company are:

_____

_____

_____

_____

_____

_____

_____

_____

_____

_____

# NOTES:

# EXERCISE 3: YOUR COMPETITIVE ADVANTAGES

This list is where you'll hang your marketing campaign. Many of your competitors offer the same benefits as you listed in the previous exercise, however you also offer some benefits that they don't. These unique benefits are your competitive advantages. Select your competitive advantages from the benefits list you just created.

TIME: 2 MINUTES

My competitive advantages are:

_____

_____

_____

_____

_____

_____

_____

_____

_____

_____

# NOTES:

# EXERCISE 4: CHOOSE YOUR MARKETING WEAPONS

This section lists the 100 Guerrilla Marketing weapons, 62 of which are free. Your job is to select as many weapons as possible from this list for your Guerrilla Marketing arsenal. Remember that marketing is any contact between anyone on your payroll with anyone not on your payroll — which means you're already using many marketing weapons that you may not even be aware of. Think about each of these weapons and make sure you select them as well as weapons that you plan on using in the future. Circle each marketing weapon that you are either using or will use.

TIME: 10 MINUTES.

| | | |
|---|---|---|
| 1. Marketing plan | 14. Days of operation | 27. Advertising |
| 2. Marketing calendar | 15. Package and label | 28. Sales training |
| 3. Niche/Positioning | 16. Word-of-mouth | 29. Networking |
| 4. Your company name | 17. Community work | 30. Quality |
| 5. Identity | 18. Neatness | 31. Reprints / blow-ups |
| 6. Logo | 19. Referral program | 32. Flip charts |
| 7. Theme | 20. Sharing with others | 33. Ways to upgrade |
| 8. Meme | 21. Guarantee / warranty | 34. Contests/sweepstakes |
| 9. Business card | 22. Telemarketing scripts | 35. Barter options |
| 10. Stationery | 23. Gift certificates | 36. Club memberships |
| 11. Outside signs | 24. Printed brochures | 37. Partial payment plans |
| 12. Inside signs | 25. Electronic brochures | 38. Phone demeanor |
| 13. Hours of operation | 26. Location | 39. Toll-free phone # |

40. Cause (environment)

41. Free consultations

42. Free seminars

43. Free demos or tours

44. Free samples

45. Giver vs. taker stance

46. Fusion marketing

47. Marketing on hold

48. Past success stories

49. Attire

50. Service

51. Follow-up

52. You / your employees

53. Free gifts

54. Catalog

55. Yellow pages ad

56. Published column

57. Published article

58. Speaker at a club

59. Newsletter

60. All your audiences

61. Offering benefits

62. Computer

63. Selection

64. Cust. contact time

65. How you say hi/bye

66. Public relations

67. Publicity contacts

68. Online marketing

69. Classified ads

70. Newspaper ads

71. Magazine ads

72. Radio Commercials

73. TV spots

74. Infomercials

75. Movie commercials

76. Direct mail letters

77. Direct mail postcards

78. Postcard decks

79. Outdoor billboards

80. Flexibility

81. Special events

82. Show displays/staff

83. Audio-visual aids

84. Posters

85. Prospect mailing lists

86. Research studies

87. Competitive edges

88. Marketing insight

89. Speed

90. Testimonials

91. Reputation

92. Enthusiasm

93. Credibility

94. Spying on self/others

95. Easy to do biz with

96. Brand awareness

97. Designated guerrilla

98. Customer mailing list

99. Competitiveness

100. Satisfied customers

# EXERCISE 5: YOUR TARGET MARKETS

The more markets where you can target your marketing, the more profits you will earn. You may have one target market, but in all likelihood you have several. The more targets you have, the more bulls-eyes you can score. Use geographical, demographic, and psychographic criteria to define your markets.

TIME: 2 MINUTES

_____

_____

_____

_____

_____

_____

_____

_____

_____

_____

_____

# NOTES:

# EXERCISE 6: BUILDING CONSENT WITH SOFT STEPS

Remember that Guerrilla Marketing is all about creating and maintaining relationships. How do you build a relationship? By creating a series of soft steps (such as free brochures, consultations, demonstrations, tours, samples, videos, audiotapes, booklets, estimates, seminars, newsletters, parties, special events, appraisals, and more) you can build trust and rapport and gain consent for more soft steps, which eventually lead to the hard step of buying much easier. You maintain the relationship by providing many more after-sale soft steps that encourage your customers to remain loyal and make repeat purchases.

TIME: 3 MINUTES

## The soft steps I will use to build relationships with my customers are:

1)_____

2)_____

3)_____

4)_____

5)_____

6)_____

7)_____

8)_____

9)_____

10)_____

11)_____

12)_____

13)_____

14)_____

15)_____

16)_____

17)_____

18)_____

19)_____

20)_____

21)_____

22)_____

23)_____

24)_____

25)_____

# EXERCISE 7: THE 7-SENTENCE MARKETING PLAN

The 7-sentence Guerrilla Marketing plan is the cornerstone of your marketing attack. In fact, most of the exercises in this book are the background research and information that will feed into your 7-sentence plan.

TIME: 10 MINUTES

1. The specific purpose of my marketing is to_____

_____

_____

2. The benefits I want to stress are_____

_____

_____

3. Our target audience is_____

_____

_____

4. The marketing weapons I will use include:

● _____

● _____

● _____

● _____

- _____

- _____

- _____

- _____

- _____

- _____

5. Our niche in the market is _____

_____

6. Our identity is_____

_____

7. Our marketing budget will be _____% of our gross (not net) sales.

# EXERCISE 8: YOUR CREATIVE PLAN

Your creative plan is only 3 sentences long. The first sentence lists the specific purpose of your creativity. The second lists the competitive advantages or benefits you'll stress. The third sentence describes your company personality. These 3 sentences will be of enormous help to you when you need to create virtually any form of marketing or public relations.

TIME: 5 MINUTES

The purpose of this creative plan is:

_____

_____

_____

_____

The benefits or competitive advantages I want to stress are:

_____

_____

_____

_____

My company's personality is:

_____

_____

_____

_____

# NOTES:

# EXERCISE 9: YOUR MEDIA PLAN

Your media plan lists whether you are striving for reach or exposure and the general media formats (such as newspapers and TV) you plan to use. This plan need not list specific media outlets. I'll get into the details of what you'll say later; for now, I'm only concerned with where you'll get the word out.

TIME: 5 MINUTES

_____

_____

_____

_____

_____

_____

_____

_____

_____

_____

_____

# NOTES:

# EXERCISE 10: CREATE A THEME LINE

Remember that the most successful and enduring theme lines have been around for a very long time. Therefore, your theme line must be something you'll be comfortable with for many years. Phrase your theme line such that is allows for expansion or diversification and include it in virtually all of your marketing. The best way to create a theme line is to list as many ideas as possible, then review your options and circle the winner.

TIME: 5 MINUTES

_____

_____

_____

_____

_____

_____

_____

_____

_____

_____

# NOTES:

# EXERCISE 11: MEME

A meme is a visual (or graphic) graphic representation that instantly communicates an entire idea. Memes can be verbal (such as "click here") or actions (such as spraying champagne after winning a race). To create a meme, think of the prime benefits that you offer, then come up with a visual or brief verbal way of calling attention to them that instantly communicates what your company is all about, even to people who have never heard of what you do. I'm giving you plenty of room for both verbal and visual memes.

TIME: 10 MINUTES

## My verbal meme ideas include:

_____

_____

_____

_____

_____

_____

## My visual meme ideas include:

# EXERCISE 12: DEPLOY YOUR WEAPONS

In Exercise 4, you selected the marketing weapons you use and/or plan to use. In this exercise, you're going to start taking your rightful control of your marketing by deciding which weapons you are going to fire when. You're not going to fire them all at once, but you must start launching a few of them ASAP.

To complete this exercise, list the weapons in the order you want to launch them, then list the exact launch date for each. Be realistic. Don't launch too many weapons at once. In fact, you may take one or two years to launch all the weapons on this list. The third item you'll need is the person responsible for launching each weapon. It may be you — and it may not. However, assigning responsibility is critical to ensure that the action gets taken.

TIME: 15 MINUTES

| WEAPON | LAUNCH DATE | PERSON RESPONSIBLE |
|---|---|---|
| _____ | \_\_\_/\_\_\_/\_\_\_ | _____ |
| _____ | \_\_\_/\_\_\_/\_\_\_ | _____ |
| _____ | \_\_\_/\_\_\_/\_\_\_ | _____ |
| _____ | \_\_\_/\_\_\_/\_\_\_ | _____ |
| _____ | \_\_\_/\_\_\_/\_\_\_ | _____ |
| _____ | \_\_\_/\_\_\_/\_\_\_ | _____ |
| _____ | \_\_\_/\_\_\_/\_\_\_ | _____ |
| _____ | \_\_\_/\_\_\_/\_\_\_ | _____ |

_____  ___/___/___  _____

_____  ___/___/___  _____

_____  ___/___/___  _____

_____  ___/___/___  _____

_____  ___/___/___  _____

_____  ___/___/___  _____

_____  ___/___/___  _____

_____  ___/___/___  _____

_____  ___/___/___  _____

_____  ___/___/___  _____

_____  ___/___/___  _____

_____  ___/___/___  _____

_____  ___/___/___  _____

_____  ___/___/___  _____

_____  ___/___/___  _____

# EXERCISE 13: BECOME THE EXPERT

The path to sales and profits is paved with credibility. You achieve credibility by becoming the expert in your subject. How? You can take simple steps to dramatically build credibility very quickly. These steps can include writing articles and columns, publishing a book, giving talks (I'll talk more about speeches later), reprints, great marketing materials, PR, and more. It is important that you give real information of real worth and value without charging and without selling (except that you can mention your company name and Web site). Determine where and how you will share your expertise, and list specific topic(s) you'll cover. The clearer you are, the easier it will be for you to establish credibility.

TIME: 5 MINUTES

## I will establish credibility and become an acknowledged expert by:

_____

_____

_____

_____

_____

_____

_____

_____

_____

# NOTES:

# EXERCISE 14: ASK YOUR CUSTOMERS

Knowledge is power. The more you know about your customers and prospects, the more effectively you can reach them and the better you can serve their needs. Remember that allowing respondents to remain anonymous lets you ask lots of important personal questions such as income and lifestyle. Make sure to ask what people like most about your company and where they'd expect you to advertise or do your marketing. List your questions here:

TIME: 15 MINUTES

1)_____

2)_____

3)_____

4)_____

5)_____

6)_____

7)_____

8)_____

9)_____

10)_____

11)_____

12)_____

13) _____

14) _____

15) _____

16) _____

17) _____

18) _____

19) _____

20) _____

21) _____

22) _____

23) _____

24) _____

25) _____

# EXERCISE 15: CREATE A REFERRAL PLAN

Guerrillas know that existing customers are the best source of new customers. They aren't shy about coming right out and ask for referrals. The best times to ask for referrals are A) immediately after the sale, B) six months later, and C) one year later. The most successful (profitable) companies have comprehensive referral plans with one or more people in charge of implementing/administering the plan and assigned dates for obtaining referrals during every year. Selling to existing customers costs 1/6 as much as selling to new customers.

TIME: 5 MINUTES

## My referral plan is:

_____

_____

_____

_____

_____

_____

_____

_____

_____

# NOTES:

# EXERCISE 16: FOLLOW-UP

Fervent follow-up is even more important than a referral plan because selling to existing customers is much easier than selling to new customers — provided you consistently provide blissful experiences. Your follow-up must be both consistent and rich with usable content. Plan to keep following-up with customers for years.

TIME: 15 MINUTES

## My follow-up plan is:

| TIME AFTER PURCHASE | SPECIFIC FOLLOW-UP ACTION |
|---|---|
| _____ | _____ |
| _____ | _____ |
| _____ | _____ |
| _____ | _____ |
| _____ | _____ |
| _____ | _____ |
| _____ | _____ |
| _____ | _____ |
| _____ | _____ |

# NOTES:

# EXERCISE 17: YOUR MAGAZINE AD

You may never run a full-page ad in a magazine, but this exercise is still superb discipline for you because, as a guerrilla, you know that the idea is king. Creating the ad means describing the visuals, designing the page, and writing the headline, sub-head, and copy. This process gives you a deep insight into the task when and if you need it. Magazines have so much credibility and reprint value that a full-page ad should probably be in your future.

TIME: 15 MINUTES

My headline is:_____

My sub-head is:_____

My graphic(s) is/are:_____

_____

_____

My copy is:_____

_____

_____

_____

_____

_____

_____

_____

*(Copy continued)*

*(Copy continued)*

46

Lay out your ad here. Don't forget to specify colors.

# NOTES:

# EXERCISE 18: EMAIL YOUR CUSTOMERS

You may want to have a professional copywriter create this email, but you should at least attempt it yourself. This email should be no more than one page to direct people to your Web site. Use short, clear words and sentences and be sure to include a direct call to action as well as very clear reasons why people want to visit your site or take the action you want them to take. Remember to think in terms of soft steps that build consent for more soft steps. The creative plan you created in Exercise 8 will come in very handy here.

TIME: 15 MINUTES

Subject line: _____

Copy: _____

_____

_____

_____

_____

_____

_____

_____

_____

_____

_____

*(Copy continued)*

# EXERCISE 19: USE POSTCARDS

Postcards are great because people can't delete them and because there is no envelope to open, meaning that your message is right in front of your prospects. Take 5 minutes to create a postcard that will support your marketing plan and make the points contained in your creative plan. Remember the call to action.

TIME: 5 MINUTES

My headline is:_____

My sub-head is:_____

My graphic(s) is/are:_____

_____

_____

My copy is:_____

_____

_____

_____

_____

_____

_____

Lay out your postcard here. Don't forget to specify colors.

# EXERCISE 20: DRAFT A BROCHURE

You may need a written brochure right now, and there's a good chance that you'll need a video brochure either now or later. Remember that print and electronic (such as HTML and PDF) brochures are great places to include all the details, and remember that audio & video brochures should be five to nine minutes long.

TIME: 5 MINUTES

My preferred format(s) is/are (circle all that apply):

print (bifold)                print (trifold)

electronic (HTML)        electronic (PDF)        video


Topics to be covered: _____

_____

_____

_____

_____

Pictures or graphics: _____

_____

_____

Color (s): _____

_____

_____

# NOTES:

# EXERCISE 21: BUILD A WEB SITE

A good Web site can provide information, contain free newsletters and other soft-step/referral/follow-up information, and even sell products and services. Your home page (the first page people see when they visit your site) is like the window display in a store: it must be visually appealing and compelling. Decide why you want a Web site and how you can profit (directly or indirectly) from it. Keep in mind that many guerrilla marketers reap great profits from sites that don't directly sell anything.

Don't forget to take full advantage of the Internet's interactivity by getting your visitors actively involved. Ask them to register for something or enter your contest — because getting their names and contact information (and consent to receive more marketing from you) is one of your biggest goals.

In this exercise, you'll sketch out your site's basic navigation, colors, heading, sub-head, and the key points you want to make. Each of the exercises you have completed so far contain valuable information that you can use for inspiration on your Web site. Why? Because all of your marketing must contain the same brand image (colors, fonts, images, messaging, and so on).

TIME: 15 MINUTES

## DOMAIN NAME

The domain name(s) (such as www.gmarketing.com) I want for my site are:

_____

_____

_____

_____

_____

_____

_____

# NAVIGATION

Use the space below to draw a rough idea of the pages you want on your site and how they will be connected. I'm including a sample navigation diagram to give you some inspiration. Your diagram need not be so detailed; just get a rough idea.

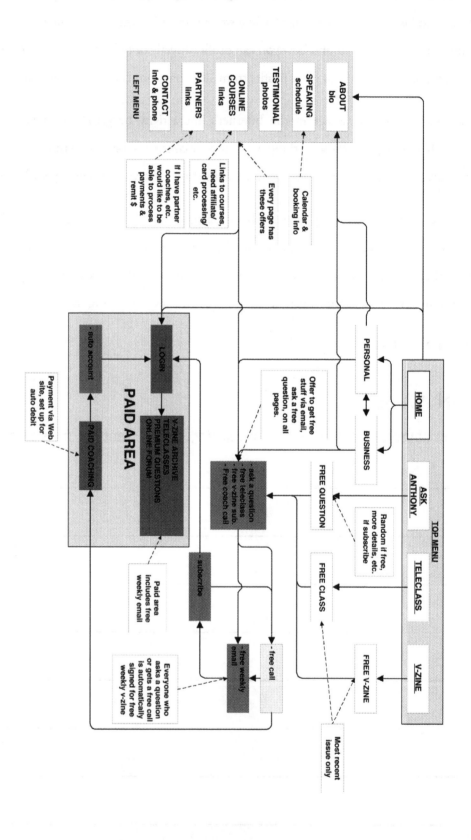

Lay out your rough site navigation here:

## LOOK & FEEL

My headline is:_____

My sub-head is:_____

My graphic(s) is/are:_____

_____

_____

My color(s) is/are:_____

_____

My main points are:_____

_____

_____

_____

_____

# NOTES:

# EXERCISE 22: YOUR GUERRILLA MARKETING CALENDAR

Your Guerrilla Marketing calendar enables you to project three years into the future and will only get more valuable as those years pass because you will be able to track your progress. Many businesses report that they need three years to come up with all A's in their marketing. Start by creating your calendar for the first year. Next year, you'll take the winners from the first year, add more marketing weapons, and keep going. You will repeat this again at the start of your third marketing year — and that is when you'll be getting your 4.0 marketing grade point average.

Remember, only complete your calendar for the next 12 months now.

TIME: 15 MINUTES

## YEAR ONE

| MO. | WEAPON | THRUST | MEDIA | COST | GRADE |
|-----|--------|--------|-------|------|-------|
| ____ | _____ | _____ | _____ | $_____ | _____ |
| ____ | _____ | _____ | _____ | $_____ | _____ |
| ____ | _____ | _____ | _____ | $_____ | _____ |
| ____ | _____ | _____ | _____ | $_____ | _____ |
| ____ | _____ | _____ | _____ | $_____ | _____ |
| ____ | _____ | _____ | _____ | $_____ | _____ |
| ____ | _____ | _____ | _____ | $_____ | _____ |
| ____ | _____ | _____ | _____ | $_____ | _____ |

## YEAR TWO

| MO. | WEAPON | THRUST | MEDIA | COST | GRADE |
|-----|--------|--------|-------|------|-------|
| ____ | _____ | _____ | _____ | $_____ | _____ |
| ____ | _____ | _____ | _____ | $_____ | _____ |
| ____ | _____ | _____ | _____ | $_____ | _____ |
| ____ | _____ | _____ | _____ | $_____ | _____ |
| ____ | _____ | _____ | _____ | $_____ | _____ |
| ____ | _____ | _____ | _____ | $_____ | _____ |
| ____ | _____ | _____ | _____ | $_____ | _____ |
| ____ | _____ | _____ | _____ | $_____ | _____ |

## YEAR THREE

| MO. | WEAPON | THRUST | MEDIA | COST | GRADE |
|-----|--------|--------|-------|------|-------|
| ____ | _____ | _____ | _____ | $_____ | _____ |
| ____ | _____ | _____ | _____ | $_____ | _____ |
| ____ | _____ | _____ | _____ | $_____ | _____ |
| ____ | _____ | _____ | _____ | $_____ | _____ |
| ____ | _____ | _____ | _____ | $_____ | _____ |
| ____ | _____ | _____ | _____ | $_____ | _____ |
| ____ | _____ | _____ | _____ | $_____ | _____ |
| ____ | _____ | _____ | _____ | $_____ | _____ |

# EXERCISE 23: WHAT YOU GIVE FOR FREE

As every good guerrilla marketer knows, there are giver companies and taker companies. This is why generosity is one of the hallmarks of guerrilla marketing. People are attracted to giver companies, and we live in the information age. What information or other valuable products/services can you give for free? Consider offering free consultations, demonstrations, samples, seminars, estimates, appraisals, delivery, installation, training, and a host of advertising specialties. The more generous you are, the more profits you'll reap.

TIME: 5 MINUTES

## The things I'll give away for free are:

_____

_____

_____

_____

_____

_____

_____

_____

_____

_____

# NOTES:

# EXERCISE 24: FIND FUSION MARKETING PARTNERS

Fusion marketing lets you spread your marketing wings while reducing your marketing costs. Also known "tie-ins, fusion marketing is coming into its own now more than ever. Form an alliance with other companies who will help you market your company while you help market theirs. Many companies have 20 or more fusion marketing arrangements, however you should start by considering only 5 companies with whom you can establish a collaborative marketing arrangement. Remember: Your fusion marketing partners must share both your target markets and your high standards of excellence.

TIME: 5 MINUTES

## My prospective fusion marketing partners are:

1)_____

_____

2)_____

_____

3)_____

_____

4)_____

_____

5)_____

_____

# NOTES:

# EXERCISE 25: GIVE TALKS

Your target market prefers doing with business with experts. One of the all-time best ways to prove your expertise and bond with your prospects and customers is to give free talks to local and regional organizations. This gives tremendous value because you'll give them real useful information that they can use to improve their lives and their businesses. Nothing builds relationships like seeing you live and in person. Remember, the aim of these talks is to tell, never to sell. Don't worry, people will remember you and will do business with you. In fact, the less selling you do, the more memorable you will be. List the organizations you'll approach to book speaking engagements below.

---

**TIP:** Not comfortable speaking? No problem. Join a local Toastmasters club, where you can practice giving speeches and can refine both your content and delivery. There are clubs all over the world. Visit www.toastmasters.org to find a club near you. The benefits are enormous and the cost very minimal.

---

TIME: 5 MINUTES

The organizations I'll approach for speaking engagements are:

_____

_____

_____

_____

_____

_____

_____

# NOTES:

# EXERCISE 26: YOUR COMPETITORS

Your competitors may not know you, but the more you know about them, the better. Information is power and you need all the power you can get. Learn about them by buying from them and seeing how professional (or not) they are. Figure out their marketing plan. Call and ask challenging questions to see how they treat you. Do they follow up after purchases? Do they have referral plans? Are they givers or takers? All of these are important questions — and the list doesn't end there. Remember that the more thorough your answers, the easier it will be to beat your competitors at their own games. List the company names only for now — you'll fill in the rest later.

TIME: 5 MINUTES

## MAIN COMPETITOR

My biggest and best competitor is:_____

The information I have about this competitor is:_____

_____

_____

_____

_____

_____

_____

_____

# COMPETITOR #2

My #2 competitor is:_____

The information I have about this competitor is:_____

_____

_____

_____

_____

_____

# COMPETITOR #3

My #2 competitor is:_____

The information I have about this competitor is:_____

_____

_____

_____

_____

_____

# EXERCISE 27: THE ELEVATOR PITCH

Pretend that you're in an elevator with your perfect target customer. You have 30 seconds to tell that person what you do and excite them about your business. At the end of the 30 seconds, they should be left wanting to know more, instead of being glad to get away from you. Write your elevator pitch here, then practice, practice, practice until you have it memorized and can deliver it in 30 seconds.

TIME: 5 MINUTES

## My elevator pitch is:

_____

_____

_____

_____

_____

_____

_____

_____

_____

_____

# NOTES:

# EXERCISE 28: TAKE SPECIFIC ACTION

Completing the previous exercises has taught you that Guerrilla Marketing is not a spectator sport. You must take action if you really want to achieve the spectacular profits you're dreaming about right now. You know you can take action because you already have taken lots of action by completing the 27 core *Guerrilla Marketing 101 Lab* exercises. This means that you are capable of taking the next required action, and the next, and the next, and the next until you achieve your goals. What then? New goals, new plans, and new action. *This exercise is the single most important exercise in this workbook for without it nothing will happen.*

TIME: 5 MINUTES

The specific action(s) I am going to take as soon as I complete the *Guerrilla Marketing 101 Lab* are:

| SPECIFIC ACTION | DO-BY DATE |
|---|---|
| _____ | \_\_\_\_/\_\_\_\_/\_\_\_\_ |
| _____ | \_\_\_\_/\_\_\_\_/\_\_\_\_ |
| _____ | \_\_\_\_/\_\_\_\_/\_\_\_\_ |
| _____ | \_\_\_\_/\_\_\_\_/\_\_\_\_ |
| _____ | \_\_\_\_/\_\_\_\_/\_\_\_\_ |
| _____ | \_\_\_\_/\_\_\_\_/\_\_\_\_ |
| _____ | \_\_\_\_/\_\_\_\_/\_\_\_\_ |
| _____ | \_\_\_\_/\_\_\_\_/\_\_\_\_ |
| _____ | \_\_\_\_/\_\_\_\_/\_\_\_\_ |
| _____ | \_\_\_\_/\_\_\_\_/\_\_\_\_ |

# NOTES:

# BONUS EXERCISE 1: 30-SECOND TV COMMERCIAL

You know that TV remains the champion of marketing and that professional commercials are very cheap. Here's your chance to create a script and storyboard for your own commercial. You have 30 seconds to get your message across. Also, many people mute the sound during commercials. Your message cannot depend on audio. I've included a sample script and storyboard. Yours may be shorter or longer s long as your message is delivered in 30 seconds. The sample storyboards are very fast sketches but they do get the required information across.

## SAMPLE SCRIPT AND STORYBOARD

Exterior beach setting. Four women sit on lounge chairs hidden behind the newspapers they are reading. Palm trees behind them. On the far left is a tanning booth standing upright.

A pale man enters from the right and crosses to the tanning booth. The women take no notice. He opens the door, climbs into the booth, and closes the door behind him.

There is an electric hum and the booth glows blue for a second. The glow fades and the man steps out of the booth, perfectly tanned. He walks off screen to the right.

As he passes each chair, the women lower their newspapers, pull off their sunglasses, and stare at him. As the man disappears off screen, the women jump up squealing excitedly and chase after him.

Fade to black with tanning salon name, address, Web site, and phone number.

End.

# YOUR SCRIPT

# YOUR STORYBOARD

# BONUS EXERCISE 2: RADIO SPOT

It's your lucky day. You've been selected for a mini-interview on a local radio station. You'll have 30 seconds to deliver a quick, effective message to your listeners — a tall order for even seasoned professionals. Jill Lublin is the bestselling author of Guerrilla Publicity and Networking Magic and a national speaker. As the CEO of the strategic consulting firm Promising Promotion (www.promisingpromotion.com), she has created successful techniques that implement bottom line results. This is her success formula:

1) State your name

2) State your relevant experience (such as "in 20 years of working in small business consulting...")

3) State a huge problem facing your specific target audience.

4) Offer three simple, fast, and effective things your audience can do to prevent or mitigate the problem.

5) Mention your Web site and contact information.

Write your radio presentation in the space provided. Next, edit and practice this mini-interview until it rolls naturally off your tongue without sounding artificial and takes 30 seconds to deliver from start to finish.

_____

_____

_____

_____

_____

_____

# BONUS EXERCISE 3: P.R. PLAN

After your product or service is available for purchase (and not before), select the newsiest elements about your offering and pick the media where you most want free coverage. You can obtain PR yourself or you can enlist the aid of a pro. If you choose to hire someone, you owe it to yourself to visit Jill Lublin's site at www.promisingpromotion.com. Her expertise will help you get the most out of your PR campaigns. Your PR plan will be for the coming twelve months. Don't worry about creating actual copy; just list your specific desired media and dates.

SPECIFIC MEDIA OUTLET                              CONTACT DATE

_____          _____/_____/_____

_____          _____/_____/_____

_____          _____/_____/_____

_____          _____/_____/_____

_____          _____/_____/_____

_____          _____/_____/_____

_____          _____/_____/_____

_____          _____/_____/_____

_____          _____/_____/_____

_____          _____/_____/_____

_____          _____/_____/_____

_____          _____/_____/_____

_____  ____/____/____

_____  ____/____/____

_____  ____/____/____

_____  ____/____/____

_____  ____/____/____

_____  ____/____/____

_____  ____/____/____

_____  ____/____/____

_____  ____/____/____

_____  ____/____/____

_____  ____/____/____

_____  ____/____/____

_____  ____/____/____

_____  ____/____/____

_____  ____/____/____

_____  ____/____/____

_____  ____/____/____

# NOTES:

# BONUS EXERCISE 4: CREATE A DIRECT MAIL PIECE

If you decide to send a direct mail piece in an envelope, you should compose a first-rate one-page letter and place it in an envelope that people will want to open — because your letter is useless unless the recipient opens the envelope.

## TIPS FOR DIRECT MAIL

Keeping these tips in mind will help ensure that your direct mail gets opened:

● Use lots of small stamps on your envelope.

● Try mailing your letters from a foreign country so people see the exotic postmark.

● Place a compelling message on your envelope that will pique the interests of your target audience.

● Make sure that the first line of your letter grabs the reader. People will read this line first.

● Always place a P.S. in your letter, because people will read that right after reading the first line. This P.S. should remind them of the key benefit of reading your letter.

● Look to your media plan and competitive advantages for insights when writing your copy.

● Always test your copy on select members of your target audience before committing to a large mailing.

● Sign letters by hand and, if you know the person you are mailing the letter to, perhaps include a quick hand-written note. This lets the recipient know that an actual human being wrote the letter, not a machine.

● Remember that people read what interests them and be sure to cater to your audience's interests.

● This letter will be part of your strategy of building consent to receive more marketing. It should ask people to take a very specific action in line with the idea of building relationships by gaining consent.

- Make sure to use as any specific facts and figures as possible and cite reputable sources so that people know you are legitimate.

- Only talk about yourself and your company to the minimum extent necessary to show that you are able and dedicated to solving your customers' needs — because that is the extent to which your customers care about you.

## YOUR TURN

Write a one-page direct-mail letter. I'm giving you two pages because handwriting takes up more room than typing.

_____

_____

_____

_____

_____

_____

_____

_____

_____

_____

_____

# NOTES:

# BONUS EXERCISE 5: YOUR GM ATTACK

In Part 13 of the *Guerrilla Marketing 101* Lecture (Disc 3), I explain how to win with a Guerrilla Marketing attack. This exercise helps you map out your own path to business victory. You have already completed most of the necessary components. Now all you need to do is go down your final checklist so you're sure you're ready to go.

For this one exercise, time is far less important than honesty. Take at least one minute to search your soul for the answer to each question, then circle the most appropriate answer. If you answer YES to all 10 questions, you're ready and cleared for takeoff. If not, then you need to go back and fill in the missing ingredients right now. Be honest, because the only person you are cheating by being dishonest is yourself. Answers for the Quiz appear on page 105.

1)  I completed all of the exercises in this workbook and done research to ensure that my answers are thorough and accurate (circle one):          YES          NO

2)  I have at least one clear and compelling competitive advantage and preferably more (circle one):          YES          NO

3)  My marketing weapons are selected, prioritized, and assigned to a responsible person for action (circle one):          YES          NO

4)  I have a 7-sentence marketing plan and am confident that it will be effective (circle one):          YES          NO

5)  My Guerrilla Marketing calendar is complete for the first 12 months after the *Guerrilla Marketing 101* program (circle one):          YES          NO

6)  I selected my fusion marketing partners (circle one):          YES          NO

7)  I have launch dates for each of my weapons and will proceed in slow motion (circle one):          YES          NO

8) I am committed to maintaining my Guerrilla Marketing attack and have the resources I need in place to do so (circle one): YES NO

9) I will measure all results and grade myself honestly each month. At the end of the first 12 months, I will select the best weapons from my Guerrilla Marketing calendar and add new ones for the second year and will repeat this process again after 24 months (circle one):

YES NO

10) I will constantly strive to improve the effectiveness of my Guerrilla Marketing attack (circle one): YES NO

*If you answered YES to all 10 questions, then launch your marketing attack.*

# QUIZ: TEST YOUR GM KNOWLEDGE

How well have you grasped the concepts presented in the *Guerrilla Marketing 101* course? Take this quick quiz and find out.

1) Guerrillas invest _____, _____, _____ and _____ rather than huge amounts of money.

2) Guerrilla Marketing removes the _____ of marketing. It puts you in control because it's simple.

3) Guerrilla Marketing is designed for _____ businesses, although businesses of every size now use its principles.

4) _____, not sales, is the guerrilla marketer's primary measuring stick.

5) Guerrilla Marketing is based on the science of _____, the laws of human behavior, instead of pure _____.

6) Focus on core competencies and core markets rather than _____.

7) Instead of trying to grow your business by adding new customers one at a time (linearly), grow your business _____ by selling more to existing customers. There are 4 aspects to this type of growth:

- _____

- _____

- _____

- _____

8) Fervent _____ is the key to success.

9) Guerrilla Marketing stresses _____ rather than competition.

10) Guerrilla marketers use _____, which instantly communicate ideas, instead of _____ that don't necessarily relate to their products, services, or companies.

11) Traditional marketing is all about the seller. Guerrilla Marketing is all about the _____.

12) Think about what you can _____ to customers before worrying about what you can _____ from them.

13) No one marketing tactic works. Guerrilla marketers therefore use a _____ of marketing weapons to promote their businesses.

14) Guerrilla marketers count _____, not just sales.

15) As a guerrilla marketer, you should embrace _____ because today it's inexpensive, powerful, and easy to use.

16) Aim your marketing at _____ rather than groups.

17) Pay attention to the _____ details of running your business, because everything you do makes an _____ (positive or negative) on customers.

18) Your first Guerrilla Marketing goal is to gain customer's

_____ to market to them.

19) Guerrilla Marketing is a _____ between you and

your customers, not a monologue.

20) Guerrilla Marketing provides _____ marketing

weapons, 62 of which are free.

21) As a guerrilla marketer, the three markets you should be working on are

your _____, your _____,

and your _____, which is your smallest but most

profitable market.

22) Devote _____% of your time and resources to the

first market, _____% to the second, and

_____% to the third.

23) As a guerrilla marketer, you are obligated to _____ the

size of your _____ and _____ markets.

24) As a guerrilla marketer, your greatest allies are your _____,

_____, and _____.

25) Your most deadly enemies as a guerrilla marketer are

_____, _____,

_____, _____.

26) Aside from profit and happiness, your biggest marketing goal is the creation

of _____ name awareness.

27) You are in 4 businesses. These are the _____,

_____, _____, and

_____ businesses.

28) Guerrilla marketers define _____ as anything that

creates profits for your business.

29) The 12 personality traits of successful guerrilla marketers are:

_____  _____  _____

_____  _____  _____

_____  _____  _____

_____  _____  _____

30)     The 16 monumental secrets of Guerrilla Marketing are:

_____ENT      _____ENT

_____ENT      _____ENT

_____ENT      _____ENT

_____ENT      _____ENT

_____ENT      _____ENT

_____ENT      _____ENT

_____ENT      _____ENT

_____ENT      _____ENT

31) Marketing is defined as _____ contact with

_____ on your payroll with _____

not on your payroll.

32) Marketing is a _____ that begins with

_____ and ends with _____.

33) Marketing is a process that has a _____,

_____, but no _____.

34) There are _____ categories of Guerrilla Marketing

weapons.

35) Category 1 marketing weapons are those that you are

_____ and that are _____ for you.

36) Category 2 marketing weapons are those that you are

_____ but which need _____.

37) Category 3 marketing weapons are those that you are not

_____ but which you _____ be using.

38) Category 4 marketing weapons are those that you are not

_____ and that you should _____

be using.

39) Use _____ Guerrilla Marketing weapons. Keep

_____ of each weapon so that you can keep those that

_____, eliminate the _____, and

build a winning _____ of weapons.

40) The most effective Guerrilla Marketing weapon, the whole point of all of

your marketing efforts is having lots and lots of _____

_____.

41) List at least three ways in which guerrilla marketers can save money:

_____

_____

_____

42) Guerrilla marketers know that people don't respond to advertising, only to

what _____ them.

43) People are (circle one)     more     less     influenced by marketing and

advertising than they think.

44) Guerrilla marketers know that poor marketing done

_____ is better than great marketing done

_____.

45) _____ are always better than vague claims.

46) When writing copy, readership falls off after _____

words, then remains constant all the way to _____

words.

47) Harness the power of _____  _____

to produce your stationery, letterheads, brochures, and so forth.

48) Three examples of memes include _____,

_____, and _____.

49) Before marketing online, you must know how to market

_____.

50) A key goal of marketing online is to grow your

_____ list.

## HOW DID YOU DO?

Check your answers against the correct answers, which are listed on page 105, and give yourself one point for each question you answered completely and correctly. Score yourself as follows:

- 50: You are a true guerrilla and well on your way to spectacular success.

- 41-49: Excellent. You are way ahead of the vast majority of business owners.

- 31-39: Good job. You've grasped many important guerrilla marketing concepts. Be sure to review areas you've missed.

- 21-30: Not bad. You may be overwhelmed by the amount of information in this course or may be otherwise distracted. That's OK, but you should re-watch the *Guerrilla Marketing 101* Lecture discs again to absorb the material before launching your guerrilla marketing attack.

- 20 or below: You're probably not ready to launch your guerrilla marketing attack. That's OK, however you need to make sure you know the theory and have a solid plan for turning that theory into action before going forward.

*Need more personalized help? Page 103 has a link to a great resource that you won't want to miss.*

# NOTES:

# COMMON MARKETING TERMS

This section contains some commonly used marketing terms and is included to help you when planning your marketing campaigns.

- **ADI (Area of Dominant Influence):** A concept that defines television and radio markets by grouping all counties in which the home market stations receive a preponderance of viewing or listening. Used in measuring the effectiveness of advertising. Can be defined on several levels such as global, national, regional, metro, urban, suburban, or rural.

- **Ad Specialties:** Useful items imprinted with the name of the advertiser and given free to prospects/customers with no obligation. Examples include shirts, hats, pens, and mugs.

- **Advertising:** Any paid form of non-personal presentation and promotion of ideas, goods, or services by an identified sponsor. May be either print or media.

  Print advertising venues include:

  - Newspaper

  - Magazines

  - Catalogs

  - Direct Mail

  - Package Stuffers

  - Billboards

  - Brochures

  - Flyers

  - Signage

  - Miscellaneous Inserts

Electronic media advertising venues include:

- TV Network/Cable

- Internet

- Radio

- Infomercials

- **Audience:** In advertising, the total number of people reached by an advertisement or medium. This number is measured by indicators such as GRP, CPM, Billing Rate

- **Circulation:** The distribution of copies of a print vehicle (including subscriptions, newsstands, controlled, and bulk delivery.)

- **Column Inch:** Standard unit of measurement of advertising space. One column in width and approximately 1/14" in depth, or 14 lines to the column inch. One column inch equals 14 agate lines.

- **Coverage:** Percent of households who receive or subscribe to a particular media.

- **Copy:** Any or all of the text elements that are part of an advertisement.

- **Demographics:** In marketing, the vital statistics that describe the characteristics of the market. Examples of demographics include: age, sex, race, religion, occupation, education level, marital status, and economic status. The demographics you must consider depend upon your target market. Sources of demographics include:

  - Internet

  - Census by geographic data

  - Survey of Buying Power

  - Sales & Marketing Management Journal

  - Media Market Guide

- **CPM (Cost Per Thousand):** The cost of reaching 1,000 of an intended target audience. Measurement of magazine efficiency. Formula: CPM = (Cost Per Page x 1,000)/circulation. For example, a magazine with a circulation of 2 million and a per-page rate of $24,000 has a cost per thousand of $12.00 (CPM = ($24,000 x 1,000)/2,000,000 = $12.00)

- **Direct Mail Advertising:** Printed (or otherwise reproduced communications) that are mailed or distributed to prospects or current customers. Key method for reaching specific audiences. Examples of direct mail advertisements, include: letters, postcards, statement enclosures, brochures, catalogs, and booklets.

- **Direct Marketing:** Direct communications with individuals to obtain an immediate response. Mail-order sales are an example of direct marketing.

- **Display Advertisement:** Advertisements that usually contain large type and/or illustrations or photographs and are larger in width than one column.

- **Flat Rate/Open Rate:** Advertising that does not offer any discounts. Usually for one-time advertising.

- **GRP (Gross Rating Points):** Also known as Target Rating Points. This is the cost per 1,000 impressions reaching 1,000 households. GRP = Reach x Frequency

- **Household Penetration:** Term used to define coverage within a geographical location. It is expressed as a percent, calculated by dividing circulation by the number of households.

- **Local Advertising:** Also known as retail advertising. Advertising placed by a retailer in a local publication or media, in contrast to general or national advertising by a manufacturer in a national or international medium.

- **Market:** Group of people who have certain common identifiable geographic, demographic, or psychographic criteria. Examples include:

  - *Geographic:* area, region, density

- *Demographics:* age, education level, occupation, religion

- *Psychographics:* values, lifestyle, involvement, social activity

- **Marketing Plan:** A written document, prepared annually, that contains the basic marketing objectives and strategies for the coming year.

- **Market Share:** Percentage of total sales of a product or industry held by one business.

- **Medium:** A vehicle for carrying an advertising message, such as newspapers, television, and the Internet.

- **Position:** Refers to the page on which an advertisement appears in the media and to the placement (left, right, top, bottom) on the page. May be Run-of-Paper (ROP) or Preferred

- **Preferred Position:** Specific pages that are considered to be prime areas viewed by readers. More expensive than ROP.

- **Promotion:** A broad term that encompasses all selling activities, advertising, personal selling, public relations, sales promotion, merchandising, and direct marketing.

- **Public Relations:** The management function that identifies, establishes, and maintains mutually beneficial relationships between an organization and the various public media on whom its success or failure depends. Acts as a voice to the media and the public. Designs activities to favorably direct the opinions of others toward the industry or the specific business.

- **Publicity:** An unpaid message that is prompted by newsworthy activities of the dealership/store. Usually prepared by the company itself, but with no guarantee of inclusion in the medium since it is unpaid. One of the many tools used by those in advertising, marketing, and public relations to generate news coverage.

- **Rate Card:** Folder published by media that provides advertisers with rates, circulation data, mechanical requirements, and other information.

- **Readership:** Also referred to as Reach, this is the estimated number of people who read a particular publication. This number differs from circulation because a reader does not necessarily buy a publication but may be a secondary or tertiary reader of a single copy.

- **Run-Of-Paper (ROP):** Advertisement placed in a publication at the discretion of the publisher (as compared to a preferred position). Basically, it is placed wherever a publisher has space for it.

- **Sales Promotion:** Mass communication technique that offers short-term incentives to encourage purchases or sales of a product or service. Examples of sales promotion tools include: cash refunds, sweepstakes, contests, coupons, samples, and other patronage rewards.

- **Secondary Coverage:** In radio, the area of the station's signal where reception is good only most of the time.

- **Signature:** A company's logo.

- **Target Market:** That segment of the market that the advertiser identifies as the people to whom marketing and advertising efforts will be directed. Determining the target audience is done by establishing geographic, demographic, and/or psychographic criteria.

- **Tear Sheet:** A copy of an advertisement "torn" from a publication and sent to the advertiser for verification purposes.

# NOTES:

# NEED EXTRA HELP?

# GUERRILLA MARKETING ASSOCIATION BENEFITS:

- Interactive Coaching Forum

- Exclusive Videos

- 21-Day Marketing Attack

- Live Chat With GMA Coaches

- Daily Guerrilla Marketing Tips

- Weekly Insider Newsletter

- And Much More!

www.GuerrillaMarketingAssociation.com

# NOTES:

# QUIZ ANSWERS

1. time, energy, imagination, information

2. mystique

3. small

4. Profits

5. psychology, guesswork

6. diversification

7. geometrically, enlarge sales, sales frequency, referrals, linear growth

8. follow-up

9. fusion marketing

10. memes, logos

11. customer

12. give, take

13. combination

14. relationships

15. technology

16. individuals

17. smallest, impact

18. consent

19. dialogue

20. 100

21. universe, prospects, customers

22. 10, 30, 60

23. increase, prospects, customers

24. customers, employees, fusion marketing partners

25. apathy after the sale

26. brand

27. stated, service, marketing, people

28. creativity

29. patience, generosity, imaginative, energetic, sensitive, constant learning, ego strength, people person, aggressive, maintains focus, embraces change, takes action

30. commitment, patient, amazement, armament, investment, assortment. measurement, consent, consistent, convenient, involvement, content, confident, subsequent, dependent, augment

31. all, anyone, anyone

32. circle, idea, repeat/referral customers

33. beginning, middle, end

34. 4

35. use, effective

36. use, improvement

37. using, should

38. using, not

39. many, track, work, duds, combination

40. satisfied customers

41. (pick any three) do it yourself, small is beautiful, form a house agency, free research, reprints, testing, stick to 1 campaign, create timeless brochures, find multiple uses, avoid vampire marketing, save $ on TV spots, market to existing customers, public domain materials, email expert

42. interests

43. more

44. consistently, sporadically

45. specifics

46. 50, 500

47. desktop publishing

48. pick any three memes

49. off-line

50. email

# NOTES:

# CONCLUSION

The *Guerrilla Marketing 101* Lecture armed you with many more weapons for the marketing wars than the average small business — and most large ones too. You just finished rolling up your sleeves, stretching your imagination, and getting your hands dirty by completing the *Guerrilla Marketing 101 Lab*. As a small business owner or person in charge of marketing, the job of acting on everything you have learned and planned falls to you, the designated guerrilla. Other people may handle this task for you in the future. In the meantime, however, it is crucial that you do them first to gain a clear view of reality in marketing. If you enjoyed the discs and enjoy completing this course, great. But that's not why I created this course. I created it to generate more profits for you. And now, you're ready to reap them.

You don't need any more motivation because by completing this course you've invested the necessary brainpower, advance planning, energy, and effort. You've made the lists and mapped out your own battle plan. You've even assigned the tasks to the appropriate people and have listed the dates for the launching of your guerrilla marketing attack. Good luck.

## Jay Conrad Levinson

*Father of Guerrilla Marketing*

# NOTES:

# GET THE COMPLETE GUERRILLA ARSENAL!

## Guerrilla Marketing for the New Millennium

A complete reworking of Jay Conrad Levinson's guerrilla "manifesto". Learn to think and market like a guerrilla and crush your competitors.

| | |
|---|---|
| ISBN: 1-933596-07-4 | Paperback |
| ISBN: 1-933596-08-2 | eBook |
| ISBN: 1-933596-09-0 | CD Audio |

## Guerrilla Marketing: Put Your Advertising on Steroids

Jay Conrad Levinson takes the proven concepts of the world's most successful companies, and synthesized them into a new type of marketing that any business can use to make mega-profits. This is Barely Legal... But You Can Still Get Away With It!

| | |
|---|---|
| ISBN: 1-933596-13-9 | Paperback |
| ISBN: 1-933596-14-7 | eBook |
| ISBN: 1-933596-15-5 | CD Audio |

## Guerrilla Copywriting

60 Profitable Tips in 60 Enlightening Minutes. Jay Conrad Levinson and David Garfinkel join forces to give small business owners, executives and marketing professionals 60 essential tactics, strategies and concepts for producing highly effective marketing messages.

| | |
|---|---|
| ISBN: 1-933596-20-1 | CD Audio |

## Guerrilla Marketing During Tough Times

Find Out Why Your Business Is Slowing Down. Jay Conrad Levinson shows you exactly why your business is slowing down in tough economic times and exactly what you can do about it.

| | |
|---|---|
| ISBN: 1-933596-10-4 | Paperback |
| ISBN: 1-933596-11-2 | eBook |
| ISBN: 1-933596-12-0 | CD Audio |

## Guerrilla Marketing 101: Lessons From The Father Of Guerrilla Marketing — DVD/Workbook Bundle

This 4-Volume set contains over 5 hours of business-building secrets personally presented by Jay Conrad Levinson, Father of the Worldwide Guerrilla Marketing Revolution.

| | |
|---|---|
| ISBN: 1-933596-16-3 | Bundle |
| ISBN: 1-933596-17-1 | DVD |
| ISBN: 1-933596-18-X | Workbook |

## Guerrilla Marketing 101: Lessons From The Father Of Guerrilla Marketing — Bootlegged

Over 4 hours of Bootlegged, CD Quality Audio, from the GM 101 Set. Never before revealed tactics and insights from the Father of Guerrilla Marketing.

| | |
|---|---|
| ISBN: 1-933596-30-9 | CD Audio |

These items are available through bookstores or directly through Morgan James Publishing at http://www.MorganJamesPublishing.com.

# NOTES:

# GET YOUR FREE GIFTS!

Until now, no marketing association in existence could make a business bulletproof. But once again, Jay Conrad Levinson, the most respected marketer in the world, has broken new ground. The Guerrilla Marketing Association is quite literally a blueprint for business immortality.

Receive a **two-month FREE trial membership** in the Guerrilla Marketing Association where Guerrilla Marketing coaches and leading business experts answer your business questions online and during exclusive weekly telephone chats. This $99 value is your gift for investing in *Guerrilla Marketing 101*.

## Join right now before your competition does at http://www.Morgan-James.com/gma.

Experience a live 15-minute telephone consulting session with Anthony Hernandez, business consultant and Guerrilla Marketing course developer. This $50 value is your GIFT for investing in *Guerrilla Marketing 101*.

Register for your FREE session by clicking on the "eye" at http://www.CoachAnthony.com.

For additional or replacement copies of this workbook, visit the Morgan James Publishing Bookstore at http://www.MorganJamesPublishing.com.

\* If you purchased this *Guerrilla Marketing 101 LAB* workbook by itself and would like to purchase the entire *Guerrilla Marketing 101: Lessons from the Father of Guerrilla Marketing* visit the Morgan James Publishing Bookstore at http://www.MorganJamesPublishing.com.

# QUESTIONS FOR JAY:

_____

_____

_____

_____

_____

_____

_____

_____

_____

_____

_____

_____

_____

_____

_____

_____

_____

_____

# QUESTIONS FOR JAY:

# QUESTIONS FOR JAY:

# QUESTIONS FOR JAY:

_____

_____

_____

_____

_____

_____

_____

_____

_____

_____

_____

_____

_____

_____

_____

_____

_____

_____

_____

_____

_____

_____

# NOTES:

# NOTES:

www.ingramcontent.com/pod-product-compliance
Lightning Source LLC
Jackson TN
JSHW052137131224
75386JS00039B/1294

# GUERRILLA MARKETING
## REVEALED!

This workbook by Jay Conrad Levinson, Father of the Worldwide Guerrilla Marketing Revolution, contains various workshop activities and projects that will propel you to business success.

The activities and projects include:

- Seven-sentence Guerrilla Marketing plan
- Developing your business goals
- Identifying and analyzing your main competitor
- Benefits list and competitive advantages
- Choosing the appropriate marketing weapons
- Identifying your target markets / nanocasting
- Business marketing meme and theme line
- Print media advertising and Radio and TV advertising
- Internet marketing principles and web home-page design
- Finding fusion marketing partners
- Developing a follow-up and referral plan
- And much, much more!

## VISIT US ON THE WEB AT:
### www.GMARKETING.com
### www.GUERRILLAMARKETINGASSOCIATION.com

Business/Sales/Marketing

**MORGAN · JAMES**
PUBLISHING FOR THE REST OF US...
www.morganjamespublishing.com

**Habitat for Humanity®**
Peninsula
Building Partner

ISBN 1-933596-18-X
90000

9 781933 596181

**Produced by Anthony Hernandez ● Design by Heather Kirk**

# IMAGINARY CREATURES
## COLORING BOOK

# JOEL NAKAMURA

**Award-winning artist and author of *Go West!* and *I Dreamed I Was a Dog***